RECRUDESCENCE

POEMS IN THE KEY OF BLACK

Eddie Bell

AuthorHouse™
1663 Liberty Drive
Bloomington, IN 47403
www.authorhouse.com
Phone: 1 (800) 839-8640

Published by AuthorHouse

ISBN: 978-1-7283-0610-0 (sc)
ISBN: 978-1-7283-0611-7 (e)

Cover Art, "Ode to the Flower Man,"
a paint and fabric collage on antique frame,
by Nellie Ashford
(Ode to the Flower Man is Nellie Ashford's memorial to honor Jessie
Campbell, owner of Campbell's Green Houses and Nursery in
Charlotte, NC, who was killed January 2016 in his Lake Wylie home.
Jessie was a friend and collector of Nellie's art. He was renowned for
his restorative work with orchids and his abiding love for children.)

Book design by Brenda May

Print information available on the last page.

This book is printed on acid-free paper.

RECRUDESCENCE

Poems in the Key of Black

by

EDDIE BELL

Including

HALLELUJAH ANYHOW

A poetic memoir

Book Design *by* **Brenda May**

—— *For* ——

ELISE GENEVIEVE
(ROBINSON) **BELL**

TABLE
of
CONTENTS

AUTHOR'S NOTE

Recrudescence is an eclectic volume of poetry, art and prose. It is the culmination of my poetic life that began sitting on the couch close to my grandmother, Juanita Carpenter Robinson, as a young child listening to her read her poetry. I was in her care after the sudden death of my mother at age thirty-five. She led me to think of the world in poetic terms. And she was black to the bone while working and writing as the lone black woman residing in Loves Park, Illinois. I have followed in her footsteps. The poetry in Recrudescence reflects race, family, and aspects of the black male experience. Women, too, play an essential role, especially my mother, Elise Genevieve (Robinson) Bell. The poetic memoir, Hallelujah Anyhow, my mother's story, was written by me many years after her death in 1942. I have no remembrance of my mother because I was only two years old at the time of her sudden passing. The piece is set during her marriage years. Her husband, and my father, was a captain in the U.S. Army, who, at the time, was away from home on active military duty. I wrote the piece as her proxy after finding a trove of letters she had written to him secreted away in his wooden WWll footlocker after his death in 1991. In one of the letters she told my father, "Eddie calls me Mama Dear."

PERSPECTIVES

How Do They See Me?

My life is a slant, a nod toward what is perceived
The watchers
How do they see me?
Is my slant an imperfection in their fashionable eyes?
A reflection of something they've been accustomed to fear?

My color, an ornament to be admired not cursed
Beauty to be acknowledged as beautiful
A rainbow's fleshy radiance
Gift of difference among sameness
No prompt for judgement or declaration of rank

How do you see me?
It's a personal thing.

Black Folk

Scene One ————————————————————

ESCAPE

Didn't want to wait to read the quilt
Wait for the railroad
Left on my own at night
All alone
Feet moving fast over stumbly ground
Then squished the swamps through soggy sucking muck
And yeah, past the snakes poised to end my journey
Had to out the lights of a vicious intruder
On the open ground free of trees and hiding places
Finally the river and I swam across to freedom
Then paused on bended knee
And thanked the Lord.

Scene Two ────────────────

MIGRATION

We left, decided, run-a-ways, though not by woods and stinking swamps
But by rail and overloaded car
On two-lane country roads
By day and by night
In fear and trembling
From home and neighboring places
A journey to unfamiliar states of tepid reception
And solid rejection
By leaving we lived, hoped and endured
And the flood continued north, east and west
To factories, brickyards, white people's home
To schools and churches, to unfit dwellings
We inserted ourselves into the American Dream
Not easily, but determined, upward we moved
Straightening our path on weary feet and with sturdy shoulders
Believing the Lord and trusting.

Down With It and Understood

I favor the inherited ways; the way brothers greet and signify
Ways we talk about ourselves, real like in abstract metaphors;
        descriptive nomenclature, cool, funny, even friendly-cruel
A language ripe with understanding shapeshifting in measured tones
Modulated words that swing a layered language brought through time
Indelible, black to the bone, stitched onto quilts beaten on drums
Spoken by brothers in places and spaces comfortable in the knowing
        that membership is real and exclusive
The club's hipness is ours alone.

Them

I feel an explanation's due
make a distinction between the Them and we,
the invidious and the called

I've sat among the mixture
heard the words of life and loathing
witnessed the purity of dung

So there's no misunderstanding
or unapplied differential thought
the Them I mean are these:

> The strident haters
> that want to be the crown,
> wear their power unmolested;
> safe, secure and full unbound

Damn the others
Those of darker hue and song
That's the thoughts they think;
that's the Them I crucify

Putting words to paper
telling truths that must be said
Reveal the lie, bring understanding
and I'll do it till I die.

Implicit Bias

It doesn't escape me
Nor do I want it to
Its lodging maintains my watchfulness
Keeps me expectant of rudeness and evil
So much a black thing, paranoia unbound
Taught to me from birth
Surgical lessons that denied a piece of me
Leaving the rest to pay the bill
And sealing the mandate to always keep watch.

Dancing by My Lonesome

Just funkin' like
Pieces of a Dream

Down with the beat
from the record machine

Swaying and movin'
dancing and groovin'

With improvised steps
One foot at a time.

Negativity Shield

I need to stop going to movies like Mudbound
They rob me of my soul and joy
I need to stop listening to sad songs
They stir unhappiness thoughts
I need to turn off the evening news
It makes me troubled of mind
       and singes my skin
So I must step away from harboring pain
The world won't miss me
And I can enjoy my view through colored lens.

Can't Stand the Feeling

Deep down lonely blues
Gets to you when you have time to think
Think about whatcha ain't got no more
Like friends that know
Friends that say what you can understand and appreciate
Lady friends that keep you knowing you're a desirable man
Getting old and gone changes things
Leaves a whole lot that memories can't fill
Makes wishing obsolete
Futility's a bitch, a sad state of affairs.

After Reading "Just Mercy"

Thinking hard thoughts in the Carolina sunshine
Thoughts that burn like passion, boil my tired blood

My tangled mind considers Them
the slavers;
the justice makers, haters flashing
their evil brand of love

Power and lucre their servant god
wolves clothed like sheep fond of preaching ungodly prayers

Thinking hard thoughts in the Carolina sunshine
thoughts of how the change must come
and when oh when we'll pay the price?

The elders walk unrested, their feet in miry clay
their spirits light upon our shoulders, whisper
Don't you hear our song?

One day we say, one day.
They mutter unconvinced and sadly fly away.

And She Called Me by Name

——— *For the sister at South State Bank*
An unexpected smile of recognition
So much time had passed, the seasons come and gone
The urban days and urban nights
The flow of life, so many in betweens
Then face to face again
Less formal than the first encounter
She spoke my name
Then casually as though the time was yesterday
She asked about my daughter; though they never met
Only a remembered conversation
I left with money and a glow
My day brightened
A poem in my heart
Life does have its pleasantries.

Sittin' On My Porch in New Paltz

My blessing spoke by Tomas
The blessing seen from where I sit
 and see what's beautiful made by God
I'm alone, a just moment
Alone to think and perceive
It's as it is
The sun is warm upon my shoulders
A comforted pleasured feeling
 that moves aside the worries of life
 and brings a godly peace.

Brown Girl Magic

Moving through a rainy day, dark clouds covering a downcast mind
      rights are all wrong and thoughts are frayed

My body moves a slovenly pace
      the bright side of life far in the distance

Spirit lost until… the pretty brown girl at the bread station
      sparkles a dumpling smile

Balance is quickly restored to proper sync as
      rays of buried sun break through.

January 19th in New Paltz

These are the pleasant moments
The quiet times that make life sustainable and at peace
The woods, expansive from my greenhouse windows
Are brightly lit and add to the silence
The ground covered in fallen leaves
Splendid, their change, their ritual of purposeful giving back
But they do as always with the turn of spring
When everything becomes new again
And a different kind of quiet speaks with pretty noise

Impetuous Act

Today I saved a life, insignificant and struggling
Unprotected in a world where small things seem not to count
And go about unnoticed, easily stepped on
Easily forgotten when hurried lives must move
The next stop waiting
So important at the time
But this day I, like the Samaritan, didn't pass by
I bent down to the rain-soaked walk
And rescued the tiny worm that lay twisting
A violent maneuver, exposed and helpless
I wonder what it thought while flying
Magically back home to the grasses from whence it came?
I'll never know if my blatantly intrusion
Paused a death wish or obligingly turned an
Ill-fated Journey.

Shrewd Dilemma

I'm dying on the inside not the out
I went where I shouldn't have gone
The museum
That had pictures and stories
Of black people, some brown
Murdered and justified
Murderers freed to murder again
I think of white folk who helped me
Loved me
I wonder is that enough?
Is the balance true and weighted?
It's the struggle that's confounding
Mind over matter
Me and the oppressor's remnants
Dancing together to a troubled song.

Brothers of the Same Cloth

———— *for Abe Jr.*

You know a friend is a friend when you call with nothing to say

I have such a friend, a universal brother of uncommon means

We walked opposing pledge lines deep in the south
       Where the campus was black and mischievous

Much later we hooked and hanged,
       The ladies and striving our constant pursuits

Life filled with youth, the slopes our thing
       Paradise lived in all colors and shades
       Until it wasn't

We've both been chopped in de-human ways
    Life made a memory, abrupt, an unwelcomed, less

But we're still here on someone else's time
    Three score and ten a thing of the past

Growing old gracefully is not our desire
    Rather we kick and damn the spoil of the piling
        Of years upon years

When too soon it must happen, just one of us left
    Life will be broken, tears will be shed

If by chance it is I
    The un-call to say nothing
        Is the thing that I dread.

Revelation — 1

Lessening

It's a humbling, quiet surprise
The can't dos, the unreasoned pains
A creeping thing that advances
No steps forward to what is left behind
Eyes seeing forbidden fruit that once hung low
        and accessible
Broken sleep, nightly trips to relieve what
        used to wait 'til morning
Mind tumbling to forgetfulness
Energy no longer taken for granted
Ordinary effort more costly
Changed conversations, truth-telling
        of life shape-shifting into a new realty:
            that what's left behind still counts.

Revelation — 2

Memories Can Be Hard (for us aging men)

Thinking back, slipping and sliding thru everything,
When young ladies were being nice and friendly
To a time you played a winning hand
It messes with your mind
Those days now past and gone
The big head knows what years have rendered
Though the little head not acknowledging a worldly truth
Remains a driven seeker of recalculated means
But it's cool I guess, the reconciliation
Knowing you've been there, had your turn
Still our eyes too willing to seek and measure
An active mind so quick to drive a foolish thought
Alas! A rude acceptance of what's done is really done
We know the train has left the station
A new day plainly wrought.

Revelation — 3

Who'd Have Thunk It

It's happening to my friends
Me
Falling apart piece by piece
Thought we had perpetuated youth
Rode bicycles, hammered Spaldines in public school yards
      Momma's denuded broom sticks our weapons of choice
Scampered across railyards with electric third rails
Sweated through grind-'em-ups to slow jams in basements dark
      Holding pretty girls tight, our bodies warm and wanting
Went to college, got educated; did our professional thing
Bouncing to and fro, the ladies, always present, made it fun
Then without warning the betrayal commenced
      Slowly at first, then like a downhill truck with no brakes
Worn out parts, hospitals, scalpels, follow-up pain
We're still moving – mind telling us lies – but at a deviated pace
Doing what we can to head off the evitable
Sure is a troubling shame!

The Last Flower

The warming air of Charlotte spring brought forth tender shoots,
      my hibiscus awakening from winter sleep

With the rising heat magnificent the blooms of pink and latent red

Each born to die too soon yet live again, abundant in ones that follow

The redeeming sequence a spectacle that cannot last,
      its time ordained by nature's pull

But then in one last gasp of showy radiance it births one solitary bloom
      that briefly sways in the quiet mid-summer Charlotte breeze

I look deep into that flower and see strength and proud endurance,
      a model for me to persevere, knowing joy awaits the morning

My life is reminiscent of that stubborn flower,
      a persistent struggle

It lasts until my season ends, though unlike this wondrous plant,
      will bloom no more until the trumpet sounds.

BLACKS

Man-Child

They called him Robby though that is not his name; he's not an abbreviation
He was cool in his overalls; dress pants too, held proper by buttoned suspenders
Country cool
Unlike city-cool Capt, who shaved with two razors, glossed his fingernails and
wore shined seasonal shoes
An earth-bound gentleman; granddad and model
Unlettered, but knowledgeable; built his own house and grew peanuts
in soil far from the south
Taught lessons from the Bible, the Law and the Testimony
Lived accordingly so I would know better how to be a man
An original brother, black and genuine, strong and upright
His name is Ellis
He farmed vegetables and souls.

Muhammed Ali

God blessed him, made him pay, then blessed him more abundantly
With keen mind, a listening soul
So filled with Allah's spirt, so obedient to the core
Yet few knew or understood his deepness
Misread his underrated love
In death we miss his water
His life revealed and amplified
Public adoration, applauded greatness
Hypocrites included in the crowd
Surely his eyes misted over then sparkled in delight
His place secure among the special
Muhammad…, the crowned; the Greatest!
Our man that understood himself, unwilling to be defined
Like David he fought among the mighty, also the common and the low
Spread kindness with his footsteps
Loved mighty; outlasted doubters one and all.

The Empire

What color is America, the land from sea to shining sea?
Not a trivial question, but one posed in search of truth

Her rich soil home to humanity only eons later wrought as theirs
      A new reality for conquerors and immigrants
          Their hue manifest and standardized
            A desperate oneness of great cost
Blood and thunder shed upon its necessary enemies
      Those of composed of vary colored skin
        Pitchy stirred into the royal pot
           For riches gain despite the taint upon the senses
            A bitter pill, yet lustful satisfaction
The times have changed, the founding fathers returned to dust

The empire casts about to remain what it is it wants to be
      But divided, as the Bible states
        It must acquiesce or surely fall
          Like Lady Macbeth, the color once planted will not out.

Time for a Changed Conversation

Shit!
We're not the 'those people' the listeners pretend to know
The ones that slide the slippery slope
Our best thrive though casually painted with the same negative brush
Harvard Princeton Yale Duke
Have seen us work our show?
Discover that brains aren't colored or white?
That when doors are cracked
The rainbow shines within
The equation is balanced, the stereotype denied
Still the story gets twisted
Too bad truth ain't as entertaining
Especially when it's black

Brother to Brother

The sun resting itself behind the clouds
Gave way to technicolor on the sidewalk
Moving with a stylized discordant walk
That suggested freedom and purpose
Though misplaced in understanding
Street creds important and in intact
The image suffers ridicule
A languid journey
Satisfied and uncompliant with the world
When he passed I spoke to a flashing plate of gold
Received a nod; an unspoken word.

Divergent Teachers

——— *(for sons and grandsons)*

Capt and Ellis men of different means
And separated ways of loving God
They saw living from opposite shores
Unlikely partners, reasoned enemies, joined by common purpose
Disparate spirits with a goal of good
Not only love, but duty drives these steadfast men of worth
One urban sophisticate, the other worker of soil
Yet teachers with knowledge of the rounders of life…
      Shinning shoes and driving cars - Homemade slingshots and planted gardens
      Waxing floors and dusting blinds – Sawing wood and dressing chickens
      Proper work and proper grooming – Flying kites and churning butter
Lessons taught and lessons learned
Two men of earthly wisdom gained of urban knocks and country toil
Their blood steel for generations
Fathers both to righteous living
Distant kin of Abraham.

Lostness

———— *(condemnation of the comfortable)*

Whose fault? The lostness, the corrupted mind
Of my brothers dear
The brown-skinned ones; untaught, unlearned
Not understanding their worth
Confused; saddened with troubled, separated minds
Those with hidden thoughts that lay buried
In un-hip hipness
Losing the ancestors extended hope
For their progeny, for fulfillment of their dreams
The ancestors walked in faith and pain
Lived hard so the next to come enjoy a higher ground
They unburdened their souls before the Lord
With praise and songs and
            fervent prayers on bended knees
Knew trouble don't last always
That joy comes in the morning
Whose fault for the now, the lostness?
The unresponsiveness, the about-face?
Judgement is present cries the witness
Lateness is at our door step and the relentless hours pass
Repent the witness cries again
Repent so the change will come.

Abscission

Where oh where have the brothers gone?
They gone a dancing one by one
Slow dragging shuffle to jail house beats
Comfortable dressed in baggy orange
The party's on at the homey's fun reunion
And ain't that just a bitch.

Where oh where have the brothers gone?
They've gone a prancing one by one
Their agile footsteps following rata tat tat
Amazing Grace how sweet the song
For a laid out brother at eternal rest
And ain't that just a bitch.

Where oh where have the brothers gone?
They've gone a steeping one by one
To beat box beat that rocks and rolls
And hardens Johnsons for "bitches and ho-s"
Leaving resultant babies and welfare moms
And ain't that just a bitch.

Where oh where have the brothers gone?
They've gone a striding one by one
Lost notes in a broken melody that plays
On and on and on and on relentless
Some dinner music for a meal of crumbs
And ain't that just a bitch.

I'm sorry for the brothers gone
I wish them back come one by one
There's so much more than slammed steel doors
No vote no job a future bleak
We're left to mourn lost hope, lost ilfe
And ain't that just a bitch.

The Statesman and the Last Concert

We're going to miss Barack
His style and class - the well-spoken gentleman
His White House rocked with soul and personality
Personage, staged and seated
      welcomed, where once they'd only served
The singers sang, the musicians played, a lasting legacy
      of soul
A boldness not seen in passing years
New history made and satisfied
The people swayed
First Lady fanned
and let folks know, It's hot in here!
Thanks Barack you've done your best
Those times were fun
We boogied from afar
But alas the party's over
And though thankful, we're left to mourn
A time that's done too soon.

The Lather

(Lath: a thin narrow strip of wood nailed to rafters, joists, or studding as groundwork for plaster).

It was a calm and early drive to Brooklyn
The old Dodge purred smoothly in the semi-morning light
and beamed rays that speared the ocean's shore

My passenger the subject of this poem?
An aging migrant, the south no longer called his home
He was thankful of my assistance driving the car he owned,
but had no license to let him take this ride alone

We rode, he talked, I listened
He spoke of work and evil practice,
one that black lathers must regularly endure

The construction site awaited, raw beams and muddied ground
The foreman privileged and greedy
rubbed his palms and spoke perversion with a grin

The lather grabbed his banded bundled
Stacked the laths against the coming wall;
each bundle counting eight, but only seven for his pay

The missing one extorted in exchange for being a modern slave
No union would accept his dues, would let him foul
the union's favored clan

Five days a week the lather hammered nails with expert hands
At day's end he stored his tools and we left the site for home
The lather's wounded pride intact and food upon his table.

Words

"A sister can hope. Don't let the brothers stop hoping"
Those were her words, borrowed and meaningful
The answer to a statement of missing
My statement - stated, meant, now reconsidered
Reminding that the prayer wheels are turning
   afar and close by
The anecdote to sadness, despair, negativity and loss
Her words kind and necessary, because she knew
   the need of my returning
     to a proper mood of faith.

Take Back What They Stole from Us
or The Lord's way is mysterious and unstoppable

Like the devil they played the thief
Taking, taking
Our freedom
Our lives
Our women
Our children
Seeking and destroying, using and deploying
Them, nasty and strained
Ungodly, godly men
Determined to earn where they did not pay
Reap from what they did not sow

But a reckoning came and comes
Recompense in due time
Disguised in form and fashion
A blindness to what goes around comes around
Redacted thinking about the physics of life

Still we claim the undeniable and make it matter
And the cost is great
On Them, on us
So it is written, so it is so
The promise is not forsaken
He will do the taking
Not from the devil
No, no
From Them.

Now She Knew and Gramma Nita Is Smiling

It was when I saw her sitting high and regal
In her box so filled with singular grace and presence
She couldn't be ignored though not among the honored
Though her name was called and eyes uplifted
Words were used that privileged her, but could not really tell her story
I had to rise to meet the vision, hear the voice
That colored the world so beautifully in song
I had to rise to tell her of the poem
The one that Nita scribed so many years ago
She invited me to sit and say what brought me to her heights
My explanation was my simple truth
To let her hear the phrase that Nita wrote
That summed the emotions of an admiring heart:
Lovely as a summer breeze, Marian Anderson that is you.

…in honor of President Mandela ——————————

Madiba's Prayer as Envisioned by Eddie Bell

Great Spirit I know you're watching me as I stumble, grow and change; always taking measured steps through foggy situations and blessing drops of rain. I serve all and feel everything; my soul bleeds in the search for freedom. I am ready to fight, ready to love, and ready to die. I came in chains to the devil's pit to be broken, cast away from other's eyes, hoped to be forgotten. But not so, Great Spirit. The ancestors bear my soul through walls of clay and transport it to the people so they fight on consumed by fire that inward burns, a driving force for righteous battle and costly toll paid without restraint for the equality of man.

I cry the unseen bitter tears of persecution and in their wake, I fortify my faith that peace will come and brother will live side-by-side with brother hands extended in friendship. The pits await me among the damned that jailers see as ragged beast, though in your eyes are your beautiful creatures made of earthly substance, sand and spit. We know of Jesus, the Christian God, and know his words are true that trials are necessary to strengthen from within.

I know not how or when I'll leave this hellish place, but the day will come when freedom's bell tolls for all and my life will be a symbol of love and equality, and the world will know a better place. I thank you for trusting me to suffer for the people in our just cause. It is fit. It is necessary. You have whispered in my ear that my suffering will not endure beyond my means.

*You strangthen me Great Spirit
so I am able to withstand.
Your love has made me strong.
It endures forever.*

Amen

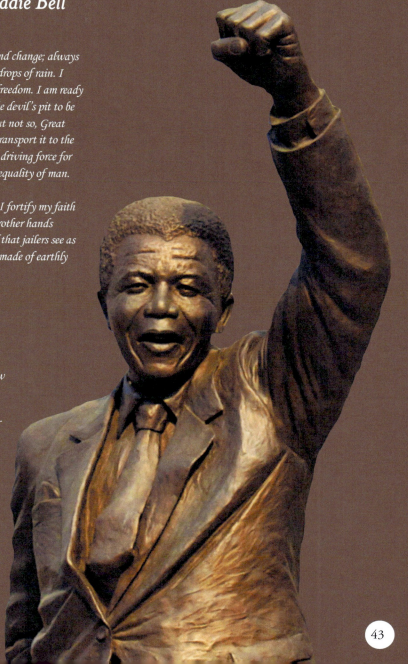

43

MISCELLANY

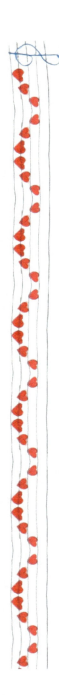

Love Music

Riffing with a lovely lady, making solemn music
Subdued notes sliding easy like
Hearts moving to the rhythms of a walking bass
And tinkling melodies like those played upon the keys
The groans of pleasure are resonating chords
Ascending bars of leavened phrases
Sounding brass of syncopated of love
That quietly fade to black
And leaves to the lovers the task of wanting more.

Got to Have Her

The lady was made for love
Somehow you know…
Her bent of badness noticeable even from afar
The pout, the stance, the willing eyes
Your psychic knowledge tells what's hidden beneath the clinging cloth
Can't help yourself
You want to taste that nectar feast of love
Relish in the promise of it all
The vibe is strong, you make your move
The seeking words unplanned
You utter them in bygone ways
Your only hope is chance.

Sunday Morning Samarians
Or They Didn't Pass By

They could have on this bright quiet day
Living their lives proceeding
Thoughts on next moments…
           church and other things
               Starbucks and a donut
Or maybe just a pleasant morning stroll
But no!
Didn't see a different color or nonexistent threat
Just stranded strangers, raised trunk and flashing lights
Instead the helping questions, kind offers to cool imagined thirst
A friendly hug, an invitation
One by one they stopped
The drivers and the walkers
Humanity on their minds
Like the Ancient on a donkey who thought it not robbery to care.

It's a Worldly Thing

Thinking of life, how it changes
A back and forth rhythm
That justifies itself even when it's wrong
Meanness sometimes at its end in disremembered truths
But then there's goodly flows reflected in the subtleness of heart
We live life's uneven precious balance
Tilted, oh so slightly, towards what it's truly meant to be.

Got Caught

Brown-skinned beauty just had to speak
Fine from tippy toe to braided hair
Sweet intelligent words came forth
from those seductive blush red lips
Perceiving her makes an old man
hate not being young any more
Glad to be reminded though
that when He feels like it
God puts it all in one package.
Yeah, I got caught looking
But it sure was nice and pleasing.

Don't Be No Fool about It

The highlife and first name recognition
Spotlights, stages, glitter all around
People wanting to hear what you have to say,
      red carpets lain afoot
And the nomination goes to…
Statues, adorned souls; effusing pride on parade
Love everywhere and thankyous aplenty
The glorious end to struggle through rough waters,
      mean streets, closed doors and doubt;
         and you're black you know,
            a factor reckoned with discernable pride
But before the stages, spotlights, and glitter
The village prayed and moved you along
      on turbulent winds
You never knew which prayer got through that
      opened that shuddered door for you
Hold tight
The village is watching and remembers.

What About Us?

The regular people, even those that receive a smidgen of fame,
     who toil in the underbrush and know the product is real and moving
The dividends long-term, seen and unseen

Recipients come back to let us know that their lives
     are full of ours,
          that they take us with them on their journey
That should surely be enough.

Black Ladies of Sparkle and Guts

Chocolate is sweeter in hued colors
especially when formed as ladies
tasteful and strong

1.
Gabby

I opened the paper and there she was
Beautiful and soaring above the beam a dollar's width
Her legs stretched skyward full and opposite
A fearless face of confidence and triumph
Winking at God as she peered toward heaven
Head and arms in graceful flight
The instant captured before descent
Blackbird flying defying the odds.

2.
Flo-Jo

Tension in the air
Fashioned glamour on the starting line
Sparkled nails flashing
Face adorned
Sparse shorts cling
Midriff bare
Body tight and beautiful
The gun explodes and off she goes
Flying hair mirroring flying feet
Stride by stride she gracefully pulls away
Her path to glory
Triumph real as scant seconds ticked away
The finish line crossed
A new standard set
Not just for winning,
But the way to look good while the deed is done.

3.
Serena

Warrior woman with an attitude
Compton's child crashed an unfamiliar world
Slowly steadily conquered sameness
Sweaty days and unknown hours
Changed the color of the script
Racket and ball
Hitting hitting
Harder harder
straighter straighter
Hood to riches fame and opulence
Pariah and savior
Queen in blossom
A warrior's spirit
Her rise determined stroke by stroke
Opponents fall, the stage grows brighter
Alone she stands at Number One.

She Made Us Dessert

———— *For Sheila Shelton*

Sparkplug
Always moving determined and instructive
Queen bee mother of twins
Raised them to be something
And they are; a legacy of worth
In her living, she struggled for breath
Oxygen a constant savior from death's stalk and wait

A call from the road, an opportunity taken
An impromptu visit quickly arranged
We sat with her on the patio brightened by sun
Talking lightly of this and that; the things of burdened life
She excused herself and then returned
            her face awash in mischievous smile
She'd planned a hasty treat, an unexpected tasty dessert!

At visit's end with unmasked hugs (no fear of germs with those she loved)
We exchanged, unwittingly,
Our last goodbyes.

THE KNIFE

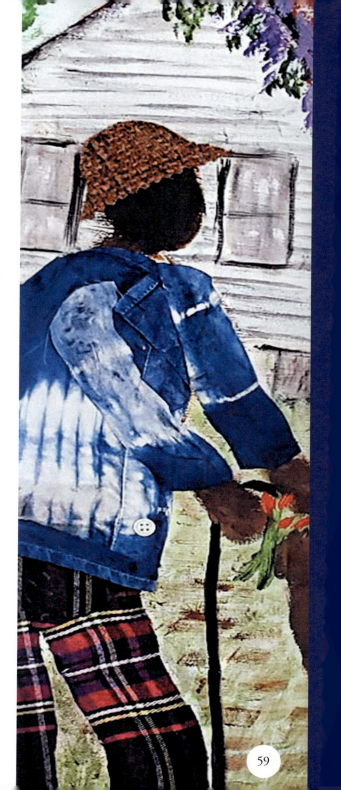

Three Hours Seventeen Minutes
to New Life and New Understandings

The event planned almost to the minute
Slicing and mending a necessary war
But that is only part of the story
The mid-point in transformation
From what contentment was to what new life brings

It's startling when an unplanned retrofit
Inserts itself into the scheme of things
Crashes the party as an uninvited guest
Takes the chief-seat in the very first row
Newcomer to the established realm

His name? you ask, well PSA, a rising interloper
Game changer and new thought maker
Signal light that blinks red and never turns to green
Bearer of bad news and counting, relentlessly
Ignore me at your peril it reads between the lines

And thus the mind reverts to what has been
Those times and years and memories
The driving force of a youthful mind
That underlying thing of sustenance and pleasure
The steaming reality inserts itself
That less will be more
Life sustained, but will it be abundant?

Enhanced Vocabulary

Kegel: repetitive contractions by a woman of the pelvic muscles
that control the flow of urine…

Didn't know that Webster Collegiate Dictionary was sexist;
or maybe just behind the times?
Men count too, especially those with prostates rudely abducted.

We men got pelvic muscles too and need to be instructed.

Upon discharge the surgeon wisely counsels:
"Do your Kegels or else be forever doomed to peeing
in your pants."

That stinks you know, an embarrassing condition.

It follows then, the cutting done and new assignment given

I'm left to morn or pursue my own ambitions.

And so I walk with knowledge now intact.

No standing pat. Engage while driving standing sitting.

Alas to leak no more and stop the flow, just practice female wisdom.

Six Month Results

Undetectable! (0.04)
That's what's known as a little less than perfect
Double zeroes the wanted goal
Blessed with reserved happiness -
> the real deal in spades
Other stuff waiting in the wings -
> should things go downhill;
> actually uphill to be more exact
Meanwhile softness still reigns –
> maybe the needle will help
Manufactured hardness, dry sensations –
> new version of manhood left to thrill the soul
Quiet prayer filled with gratitude –
> near double zeroes much better than the digit 1
Thank you, Lord, for your mercy
Gives a brother some hope.

Awaiting Kegel Redemption

I grow weary waiting for the end to come
The throwing away of bloomer and pad
No longer needed to stop the soil
No longer needed to feel safe, protected from an awful shame
Hope flickers bright then dims when least expected
The dam gives way, the prize unreached
Tomorrow's promise yet to be fulfilled
In slavish obedience I persist
What other choice have I?
My burden born in secret
An unwanted companion keeping me afloat
Until my blessing comes.

Aftermath (Sitting alone in Freedom Park, Charlotte)

The cutting done, the evil rooted out
A void created and naked truth exposed
All must change, a managed physicality
Shifted frame of mind
Both fragile, both a mystery
How will the new life be?
The surgeon's knife, a two-edged sword
Cuts tissue and emotion
Creates a negative assortment
Maxi-pads, diminished manhood
Meaningless memories left
To manage the loss of youth
But ah the wait for Grace
And removal of the thorn
Leaves time to read and contemplate
In what better place than a park named Freedom
A place where even God can rest
His creation passing, moving by
           in sync with pleasant undertakings.
A day of abandon in the warmth of Charlotte's summer sun.

Stumbling Block – One Year Later

Near perfect no more
Rising like a cool breeze that
Leads an approaching storm
The monster is loosed and roaming
What does it mean?
Who has the answer?
The next test is coming
An understudy waiting in the wings
The thorn still in my side
Will grace be sufficient?
And so, I continue to deal and wonder
Living life until the living's done.

Aftermath Part 1 (Help Doc McStuffins)

It's the dread that I feel
Though innately I seek the promise
The drudgery persists through the flash of days
And the midnight of darkness
My thoughts are skewed and unrepentant
They move from things that were
To things that may never be again
Is a man's worth measured by hardness?
I think not yet, who can judge?
The reckoning comes with failure
And the leavings short of passion
Left flaccid and ashamed
The failed test, a plague that drains
And keeps one's life asunder.

Aftermath Part 2

The machine and its rays of radiation,
Necessary
Chases evil cells missed by the knife;
Scavengers prowling to seek and destroy
The machine whirrs and buzzes
Squeals
Back and forth it hovers and circles
Flashes squiggly green lines across the ceiling
I lay mummy-still and listen to its language
Learn its intonations
It's familiar now
I speak it silently
Sixteen months have passed since the cutting
Rising numbers the machine's initial cue
In minutes it's over
I rise and dress, rush to free my bursting bladder
Twelve days down, twenty-five to go.

Shooting Blanks

Not like the movies and rata tat tat
More subtle; less dramatic
The kind of which I speak is post-removal
Those sensual ones that ain't for real
Not like those that empty and fill
Just half a loaf this substitute blessing
The real feel without the leavings
Faking it like you making it, so to speak
Can you dig it?
No?
Neither can I.

It Ain't As Bad As You'd Think
Or Johnson's Second Chance

The needle and its destination
A sacred place, "Johnson"
laying softly in-wait
Oh to stand tall again!
Ultimate messenger that both gives and receives

The compounder makes his magic elixir
Manhood in a vile and next the pudding-proof
A trial execution

Drawers off, the sacred place in view
Unabashed, the nurse instructs:
Pull Johnson to full extension
Swabbed him clean,
Fill the needle
Yes, there's the spot

Trembling hands fumble, stick and plunge
Message and wait and watch
As slowly rising Johnson stands erect
His ninety-minute reprieve.

Got Enough?

Is that possible?
The manly question, paramount consideration
In the way of things
The flippant response so easily rendered pointed and instructive -
"If God made something better He kept it for himself"
A truth in the main and the pursuit self-justified
Hittin' & missin' seeking and catching
Participating in the righteous sanctioned gift
Triumphs to be remembered and forgotten
How then regard the rising PSA monster
Inevitable reckoning that slants the gift
And worries the mind with imposing thoughts of failure
Choices are offered against the bleak assumption
"Watchful Waiting" keeps things at bay for yet a little while
But in the end
It complicates the answer.

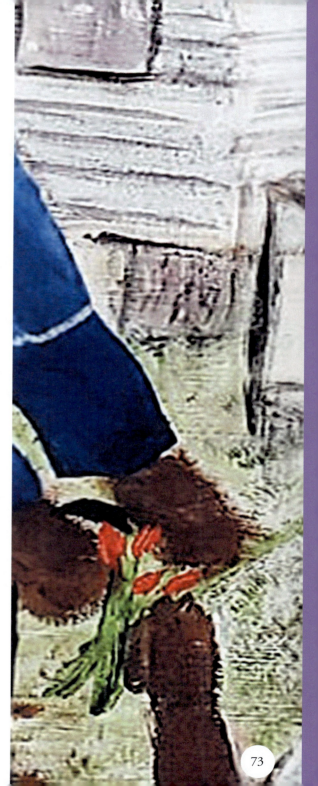

MAMA DEAR

Mama Dear: A trilogy

1.

TAKEN

I knew her once as a child knows from whence he came
The bond formed of blood, the substance of unborn life
I suckled at her brown-nippled breast and found it sweet I'm told

She hummed to me the spirit words learned of bygone days
Times of suffering in the unyielding heat of sun drenched fields
Her melodies pressed softly upon my heart, they sing to me yet now

Too soon she left to rest in deepest earth, took before her promised time
A leaving I have suffered since; an emptiness void of smell or softness of a kiss
And unremembered icy tears shed against that act of fate

The silenced sounds from Mama's lips; the chasm dredged too wide
      and deep to fill
She died before I knew her name; damned heart that wrought the stunning pain
And tore to shreds the bond of mother-love imagined only,
      but never to be known.

2.
A SOLILOQUY OF NO

No dreams of ghostly visits from the grave or sightings in the flesh
No stories told of height or of the color of her hair
No mention of a lonely life or longing for an absent man
No recounting of her favorite foods or how she held her fork
No talk of school, no talk of trade or expertise
No rendered poems from poet mom to please, inform, delight
No stories for the little me who wondered where she was
No sad-filled words to tell the lost-ness tale of cruel and deep
No nothing of her spoken ever. 'No nothing of her, please.'

3.
LETTERS

I read the letters kept furtively stashed among decaying things
Why kept these alone that told and asked of ordinary life?
Surely there were others that he read and discarded uncaring in the trash

Why these indeed that proved to be her final written words
I cannot know the mind of God though I recognize his hand
Mercy granted, mercy given, it had to be God's plan

I knew of the battered dirty wooden trunk asleep on the basement floor
It wrought no thought of treasure hid within this survivor of the war
Just one more task that need be cleared when death relieved his unrepentant life

In due time I ventured to see what illuminated secrets lay inside that trunk
And there they were the letters, secure and neatly ribbon bound;
my heart, my breath, my unbelief…
I read her words that left me weak and flew at me as signs of grace

I read my name on the tender paper plainly scribed by Mama's hand
She wrote in words that spoke of me; a mother's telling of a pleasing child
A baby son of limited words who called her Mama Dear

So there it is, that chasm deep and wide exists no more
It's filled with thoughts and nightly dreams of when I'll see her face-to-face
My soul so long in grief is finally gratified.

HALLELUJAH ANYHOW: *A Poetic Memoir*

How did I know that life would be a slippery bar of soap
submerged in the bath tub, moving just out of reach at the
touch, dissolving before it can be properly used up?
Not just any bar of soap either.
Surely not Ivory (99 and 44/100 % pure),
more like Octagon, its lye burning while it cleans.

Don't know what happened.
Didn't know I'd be an unlearned memory, a wish,
a crutch, the text of a poem.
Certainly didn't want to be my mama's sorrow.
I heard her crying in the attic wishing it was her.
Couldn't be though - wasn't her time.

I was lovely enough, almost pretty
as Elizabeth, except for these long legs.
We was a pair, we was.
Strutt'n around like we was the cat's meow.
There were beaux a plenty then
and rides in pretty cars.
Mama scolded us about our flounc'n,
she didn't take kindly to floozies
or loose living.
We was proper Negro girls,
not po'white trash.

It's hard to scratch a missing-mother itch.
Just as hard to dream a touch that makes a baby smile.
        I was two when they stopped me at the
door. Shut me away from a sight they should've
let me see. Sleep'n is not a strange thing.
She was just still (and natural)
like when she dozed as I nursed.

        Mama had a fit when I told her.
It was at the Bud Billiken picnic in Grant Park.
Told her right out, "Mama I going to marry
that Lieutenant, he so handsome and smart
I just know that he'll be good to me.
When he calls me his darling baby girl,
I gets all warm inside."

She never was the same after that.
Wisdom can be a hurtful thing.

        I stopped crying after a while,
guess pain is short in babies. Gramma Nite
used to sway me on her lap in the bathroom,
loving Mama and me with her lullabies.
Later she read me her poems and
told me stories, but never one about Mama.

Being innocent has its good points,
but it didn't help me much with Capt I guess the
Depression made us both strong, only he came
out of it a worldly my-way man.
I couldn't understand his kinda love.
He left me too much time
for dreaming and not enough for the
real thing.

"It is not all of life to live,
nor all of death to die.
Time hurries past thee like a breeze...." (unknown)

       Capt didn't know I was going to die.
Maybe if he had, he wouldn't have gone off
and left me alone with those two boys.
They kept me plenty busy,
especially that older one.
Junior had a mind of his own.
Used devious means to let me know
that he was around.
He had a way of thumping
Eddie so I'd pay attention.

Mama, 1 read your letters, the ones
you wrote to Daddy in 1942. Did you leave them
for me to see? Maybe not, because it was Daddy
who kept them in that old wooden trunk.
They are the words I never heard you speak.
You wrote my name! An ordinary thing
in an ordinary letter; yet a treasure,
something to cry about.

Sure am a lucky girl to have two boys.
Mama, 1 read your letters, the ones
you wrote to Daddy in 1942. Did you leave them
for me to see? Maybe not, because it was Daddy
who kept them in that old wooden trunk.
They are the words I never heard you speak.
You wrote my name! An ordinary thing
in an ordinary letter; yet a treasure,
something to cry about.
Sure am a lucky girl to have two boys.

Most women feel blessed to have just one.
Now Junior, the frisky one, is smart (an stubborn)
like his daddy and don't take well
to scold'n. Capt don't either, gets sad
as hell on those occasions when I get my nigger up.
Eddie Derrick's just a baby,
but he learns quick like his brother.
Likes to be cuddled;
got two genes for affection like me.
Only two, an already call'n me Mama Dear!
Ain't that sumpth'n?
Junior will get the gals with his gab,
Eddie will sweet'n them to death.

January 12th, 1942

My dear Hubby,

You may never read this letter
darling, because I not sure I have
the courage to mail it. I must
write it though, for me, because
for months now there has been a certain
kind of urgency inside me which
I can't explain, but is there
nonetheless. Maybe it's at the
root of my crazy acting you told
Mama about.

I was so happy when we were
courting, like when I was a
little girl daydreaming on the attic
floor. You were so confident
and selfassured.
There was always
something missing in those boys
from South Rockford. Oh we
carried on some with them, me
and Elizabeth, but I just couldn't
wait to move to Chicago and
meet some dignified men. I guess seeing all
those beautiful gals and dapper
guys in the Chicago Defender got

me hooked. Then out of
nowhere you walked in to that
party and I knew I'd seen
something special.
When you asked me to dance I
was ready. Boy didn't we cut a
rug that evening! Nobody had
ever moved me around the floor
like that before. Seemed like the
movie, me two-stepp'n with a
handsome, suave, gentleman
soldier. I think I showed off a
little bit for my girlfriends, 'specially
Elizabeth because she is so pretty
and the boys always look at her first.
Did you?
Well after that party I
knew that I was in love. Took
a while for it to take shape in my mind, but
my heart knew it right away.
I was a scared Momma that I met a
Chicago boy at the
party, a lieutenant! She was
irritable with me after she met you.
Said that sweet-smelling men
who slicked back their hair
and polished their fingernails
couldn't be trusted. "Lowdown
Army men only use to them low-life
street curs. Don't appreciate a fine

Christian woman with good
upbringing." You know we
never changed her opinion of you very
much, but I was grown and
did what I wanted to do.
Now that we're married
and have the boys, you are
gone, wonder sometimes if Mama
wasn't right. These eight
years have been a struggle. Trying to make
ends meet and trying to
understand you. I never used to worry
much when you were out late
galavant'n around with you
soldier friends. Maybe I
should have?
But the ache of loving you is
always strong. I miss you so
much right now. Baby, why
can't you be here and why
don't you write or call?
You know how devoted I am to
you, but I'm worried sick honey.
Deep down I can feel that you
have another woman. Is she pretty?
Are you going to leave me?
How can I go on!
I don't feel good all of the
time. Seems like I don't have
much energy and or patience.

Mama's being hateful, always running you down in front of me and the boys. Daddy chimes in too, saying you're a whore monger and no good. It is hard to keep faith in you baby. I want to though. I want you to real bad. Oh my God baby just come home and take away all this pain.

Love, Elise

84

Where does the fault lay that I know
little of you, so little
as to really know nothing at all?
I ate at your table, slept in your bed,
heard the voices that comforted
your crying, and of you
I know nothing at all.
I picked where you picked,
cut grass that you walked upon,
cultivated the garden
that nourished you, and yet of you
I know nothing at all.
I walked past your grave on the
sabbath, listened to lullabies
that caused you to sleep,
lay on the loins that birthed you,
still of you, I know nothing at all.
I heared cries from the cups my brother,
teachings from the lips of your father,
and lectures of life from my daddy;
but about you, I know nothing at all.
No, nothing at all. All this, and I
know nothing at all.

"Death angel flew by again girl,
at least that's who I think he is. He
was in my dream, stared at me like
he was trying to figure out if I
was the right one.
Strange I should recognize him."
"Damn it Elise, it was just a dream,
just a missing your husband
lonely wife dream."
"Mama told me that if I married Capt,
I die of a broken heart. He's a low
down gutter nigger with gutter ways,
was the rest of what she said.
Funny though, there is a strange feeling
in my chest from time to time,"
"Go on girl. It's just worration."

"You probably right, it must be the
loneliness. Must be...."

Time has passed Mama
and things are better. You can see,
can't you? The old, reborn in the new
and kept young through blood and
stories. And the pictures are on the walls,
all the players of our heart
strings. The sowers, the fertile ground,
the harvest. Jesus spoke of these
things. So do the pictures, Mama.
Junior kept them, are you proud?
Today it is as it is
supposed to be, the living, for the
living, not the dead. Memories of
gnarled sin reproved, forgiven,
understood, covered forever
by wisdom and light; not cast away,
because the lesson must be taught
(and learned) that hurt is not justifiable
reason for harm.
Time, more generous to me
than you, is catching me and winning;
and so it should, but after the angels
work with me, there will be stories
of you and your lieutenant and
the rest of us.
And Mama Dear, Hallelujah Anyhow.

Epilogue

Elise Genevieve Bell, the writer's mother, died January 24th, 1942. She never received the reply to her letter of January 12th to Capt, who was on active military duty in Seattle, Washington. His letter, written the same day that Elise suffered a fatal heart attack, arrived in Loves Park, Illinois several days after her death. That letter was opened and read for the first time by her youngest son, Eddie, on March 16th, 1996. The letter began-"My Darling Wife" and was signed: "With Love/ Remember, C".

The following is a poem written by my maternal grandmother, Juanita Carpenter Robinson. It was published in Sampler, a publication of the Rockford Writers Guild, circa 1950.

The Little Dark Angel

———— *Written by Juanita Carpenter Robinson*

The little dark angel came to the gate.
"St. Peter gwine be mad 'cause ah'm late,
An' ah hurried so fas', now ah'll jus' res' mah feet,
Befo' ah mus' walk the golden street."

He sat down to rest. It was quiet here;
The sun was so warm, the air so clear.
He could hear laughter, and bursts of song
And whispers of footsteps, so ere long
The eyelids covered the dark eyes deep,
And the small dark angel fell asleep.

St. Peter opened the portal wide,
Awakened the small one, and took him inside.
"St. Peter, ah'm sorry ah'm so late."
St. Peter smiled gently, and closed the gate.

About The Author

Eddie Bell acquired his love of poetry at the knee of his poet grandmother, Juanita Carpenter Robinson. Many years later he went on to hone his craft at residencies at Ragdale Foundation in Lake Forest, IL. He has published three previous poetry collections and his work appears in numerous literary print publications. A highlight of his writing career is his three reading tours in Paris and Central France. He is an eclectic writer and has significant nonfiction and freelance journalism credits. He is a New York transplant residing in Charlotte, NC.

Artistic Credits

Nellie Ashford is an African American folk artist based in Charlotte, North Carolina. She is a self-trained artist whose primary works are mixed media collages featuring paint and various cloths, many of which have a historical reference. She has exhibited widely throughout the Carolinas, including the Levine Museum of the New South, The Harvey B. Gantt Center for African-American Arts + Culture and the Mint Museum Uptown, both in Charlotte. Ode to the Flower Man: Cover art.

Ron Moultrie Saunders is a San Francisco based photographic artist, landscape architect, teacher and public artist. He creates artistic photograms: photographs that are made without the use of a camera. His artistic focus is personal, explores relationships, and his place in the world as a black male with Jewish, African American and Native American roots. His work has been exhibited throughout the United States, including the San Francisco International Airport, Corden Potts Gallery (San Francisco), Middlesex County College (NJ), and the Oakland Museum of California at City Center.
Photograms location - Pages: 25, 65, 67-68.

Midge Monat, a retired elementary school teacher, is a painter and watercolorist based in Bloomingburg, New York. In addition to working in watercolor, she also works in oil and is an accomplished maker of batik scarves. Her work has been exhibited at various venues in the Mid-Hudson Valley area (NY) and at the Northeast International Watercolor Society Show, Kent, Connecticut.
Watercolors location - Pages: 16, 19, 23, 30, 49

Eddie Bell is a writer, poet, and photographer, formerly based in New Paltz, New York, but now residing in Charlotte, North Carolina. He is the author of four poetry collections. His photographs have been exhibited in the Bronx Museum of Art (NYC), Mohonk Mountain House (New Paltz), and the corporate headquarters of Phillip Morris. His work also appears in newspapers, magazines, newsletters, the cover of the Ulster County (NY) Yellow Pages, and in an issue of the Professional Photographers Annual. Photographs location: Front cover; and Page: 83

Other Credits:

Statue of Nelson Mandela at the Groot Drakenstein prison near the town of Franschhoek, Western Cape, South Africa. Photo 12970963 © Gail Benson - Dreamstime.com

Thank you to my friend Jessica Battle for her special contribution and to all of the artists whose contributions have made this book unique.

Other Publications

"OUR CHILDREN'S KEEPERS" ©2013

"Our Children's Keepers" is a guide for the development of successful group pre-college mentoring programs. It deals directly with program planning and administration, as well as the roles and responsibilities of mentors, parents, and students. It is also a resource guide for families with high school students preparing for college admission.

"EENY MEENY MINEY MO, TIME TO LYNCH A NEGRO" ©2009

This daring book is a collection of free-verse poems and short stories that elicits a tapestry of emotion as it reveals the humanity of lynching in a unique, memorable presentation. Though the subject matter is disquieting, it is handled with grace and thoughtfulness and will leave the reader moved and with a deeper understanding and appreciation of this part of the American story.

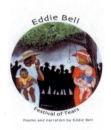

FESTIVAL OF TEARS: POEMS AN D NARRATION BY EDDIE BELL ©2009

A dramatic presentation of poetry that brings together jazz and classical musicians rendering Negro spirituals and jazz improvisations that accompany Eddie's harmonic voice and add depth to the recording.

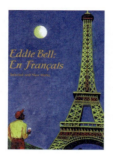

"EDDIE BELL: EN FRANÇAIS SELECTED AND NEW WORKS" ©2003

Eddie Bell's second volume of poetry, is a compilation narrative poetry in English with side-by-side translations in French. The translations in this unique book were accomplished by a task force of accomplished French poets, French English professors, and French students. Some of the poetry is taken from *"Capt's Dreaming Chair,"* with a few of the poems drawn from Eddie's experiences in France. One poem, *"Side Streets,"* was presented to President Bill Clinton at the White House. President Clinton had this say about *"Side Streets"* in a letter he wrote to Eddie: "We want to thank you for the poem. It's wonderful, and we will treasure it all the more because of the history you helped make possible..."

"CAPT'S DREAMING CHAIR" ©2001

"Capt's Dreaming Chair" is Eddie Bell's first volume of poetry published in 2001. This collection of narrative poetry tells human stories about life situations. Many of the poems are taken from the lives of his family, especially his father, Captain Carl Bell, a self-made man, veteran of two wars, and family patriarch. The poems take on a universality that crosses cultures, ethnicities, and ages. When Eddie reads them in public, it is not uncommon for emotions to tingle and tears to flow in recognition of life's unfair circumstance.

Website

Visit the following website for more informaiton or to
purchase any of the books listed under "other publications".

www.eddiebell.com

Contact Eddie

Via email: eddiebell@carolina.rr.com

Engage Eddie Bell for Your Event

Eddie Bell is available for readings, lectures and workshops at schools, colleges and universities, churches and literary events. His many appearances include being a featured reader at The Poetry Project at the venerable St. Mark's Church in New York City, guest reader at the City College of New York's Poetry-in Performance, and was poet-in-residence at Cal State San Bernardino, CA. His substantial resume also includes three sponsored tours of Paris and Central France where he appeared at select venues of educational institutions, a Paris jazz club, public library, and a wide variety of community events.

Contact
eddiebell@carolina.rr.com

www.eddiebell.com

Printed in the United States
By Bookmasters